JENNIFER HUDSON GORMER

kidCEO™

Amazing Kids Share Their Success In Business!

Foreword By K. C. Fox

Layout and design by
BLI Publishing, Dallas, TX.
1910 Pacific Avenue
Suite 7024
Dallas, TX 75201
www.BLIPublishing.com

To order
Idea 2 Profit
1601 Elm Street
Suite 3300
Dallas, TX 75201

Printed though Ingram Spark.

Printed in the United States of America.

ISBN: 0-9988802-3-X

FOREWORD

In order for a child to dream and dream big, they have to be given the thumbs up that it's okay to dream, next they must be given the high-five and freedom to chase those dreams, and finally they must be awarded the foundation, the training ground that proves those dreams are realities waiting to present themselves.

Back in my day, prior to Twitter, Facebook and Instagram serving as top tier elements in the world of marketing, sales and revenue, the outline was as follow:

- Go to school
- Pay attention
- Do as you are told
- Stay out of trouble
- Get a decent job

Yeah, yeah, I'm with all of the above, but most importantly the powers that be forgot to tell us to expose and expand. They forgot to tell us to practice free thought and they forgot to educate us on the deeper routed elements of economics and free enterprise. Now here we are in the 21st century, where technology is the number one driving force in business and financial freedom. It is the vehicle of e-commerce, small, corporate, and conglomerate businesses alike, all across the nation and internationally.

As a small-town skinny Black girl with big lips and a mediocre education, at best, the aspirations of being an entrepreneur never made the cut for 'fire-side chat" in my household or in my school for that matter. It wasn't backyard or front porch talk over watermelon amongst the neighborhood kids in my hood. It wasn't that I thought it was unattainable, per se. It was more of the fact that I had no idea that it was even an option. I often wonder who's to blame for that in my adult life.

Being an entrepreneur has its challenges in general. Can one even imagine what it's like striding and striving for entrepreneurship as a double minority? I know firsthand the overwhelming woes that will knock you over the head at every turn while working towards that startup you've dreamed about for years. If these are my experiences as a 40-year-old Harvard educated woman, one can only imagine how these challenges will rear their ugly head to the ambitious 13- or 14-year-old girl or boy with a big smile and trusting heart.

If you are reading this, chances are you, too, have taken on some new friends as of late.

As we pass the baton and fall to the rear as veteran entrepreneurs, it is important for us to mentor, enlighten, and highlight those who will continue to advance our economy and quality of life with business education at the forefront. Part of that entails embracing the ideas of those younger generations. In a recent conversation at the offices of the master of business and business development himself, Daymond John, he and I chatted about the business future of a 19-year-old destined to be great. At one point in the conversation, Daymond looked up and said, "But what does the kid want to do?" While passing the baton it is imperative that we embrace the same freedom of thought that we once craved.

The kid authors/entrepreneurs in this anthology are in a uniquely blessed situation. It's not every day that you get to perform under the auspices of a best-selling author that has literally defied the odds of entrepreneurship all while being wrapped in a double minority cloth. In the introduction, I mentioned training and foundation as the vessel for free thought and dream chasers. Jennifer Hobson Gormer brings an exhilarating authenticity of those elements to this anthology by way of her interaction with the X, Y, and millennial generations through her time as a collegiate professor as well as running a successful business development company in one of the fastest growing cities in the nation. Her ability and keen insight into an era where entrepreneurship is the new way of life coupled with her 20 plus years of experience as an educator and business woman, makes this anthology very relevant and compelling.

Penning this foreword has become one of my proudest moments. Not proud of myself per se, but overwhelmingly proud of those young trailblazers for their tenacity and global visions. At times, it's hard to notice the wins when there are so many losses flooding the airwaves. For these young entrepreneurs to identify themselves through business and service, speaks to the power of the 21st century and the emerging leaders at the helm.

EXTRAordinarily Yours,
K.C. Fox
Media Executive Top 5 Market
President Vaulted: The Lady General Foundation
SVP The Vault Consulting Firm
CEO TLG Group
2ND VP NAACP

MEET OUR kidCEOs™

INTRODUCTION

Imagine being a teacher, mentor, parent, aunt, or relative of a child who had a dream but had no idea of how to make that dream come to fruition. Imagine that same child, being able to dream the impossible or achieving that 'thing' they dreamed of despite having never seen anyone in their life do that 'thing'. Imagine a child with hopes of surviving their own circumstance, or making a better life for themselves and their family. Imagine that child wanting to stretch themselves and learn, and give their time, energy, and resources to fulfill their dream. Now, imagine that child's eye twinkling with hope, smiling with aspiration, and standing with courage.

This is the story of every kidCEO™ in this book. Each kid, under the age of 20, had a dream and made a decision to go after it. That dream was to become a CEO of a company. Each one of the kids in this book will tell you how they dreamed of their business, identified their passion or purpose, and did the work to start, launch and now run a successful profit producing business. I searched the country looking for kidCEOs™ who were defying the odds, and I found them.

Becoming an entrepreneur is not easy. It takes hard work, perseverance, and dedication. From writing a business plan, developing business strategy and growth plans to building a brand, and selling products and services; entrepreneurship has caused many adults to throw their hands up and work for someone else. But not the kidCEOs™ in this book. Like me, they have done the work to start and run their own business.

I am a serial entrepreneur, thanks to my mother. At 15-years-old, I started my own business as a freelance choreographer and dance teacher. I worked with non-profits, school districts, and private dance studios. I learned how to run a consulting business and my accountant taught me about the IRS. I learned how to write a profit and loss statement and how to track my mileage and expenses. I learned what my time was worth and how to charge appropriately for the value and services I offered.

I opened my own dance studios after graduating with my Bachelor's degree in dance and was highly successful. I had some huge successes but I also had some huge failures. I actually learned more from my failures.

For exampes, the importance of budgeting in business and why you need a team. I learned how to minimize my expenses, the importance of debt to income ratio, and to develop my own brand. From owning my studios, to becoming a Mortgage Loan Officer/Broker and Learning Consultant to the world's most successful billion dollar brands, I have managed several successful businesses making six figures from my early 20's to my 30's. My passion has grown into helping other entrepreneurs grow their businesses and to avoid making the same mistakes that I made.

Now, as a mother of a kidCEO™ myself, I will never forget the day that my daughter walked into my room at the age 11 and said, "Momma, I want to open up my own design store." Within a months' time, my daughter opened her small 10 x10 store in an antique mall and almost ran out of inventory within hours of opening. I was so proud of her, and I made a promise to myself to do what my mother did for me, for her.

kidCEO™ is not just a book. kidCEO™ is a resource for both kids and their parents alike. I have met many kids who want to start a business but have no idea how to start. I have even had discussions with parents who didn't know the first thing about how to support their kids. I have even overheard parents tell kids they were crazy for stating they wanted to start their own company. It broke my heart.

That is why kidCEO™ exists. In this book you will hear from kids about how they discovered their passions, identified their purpose, and the steps they took to start and open their business. They will even share the lessons learned from both their successes and their failures. Lastly, each kidCEO™ share Keys to Success for other kids that are on the same journey and need a little help.

This book would not be complete if we did not hear from the parents behind each kidCEO™. I firmly believe that behind every great kidCEO™, there is a supportive parent helping that kid make it happen ; not doing the work or running the business , but guiding , supporting , and helping their kidCEO™. So you will hear from the parent behind the kidCEO™ about what it takes, and what they have had to do, to help their kidCEO™ achieve their dream . Our goal is to encourage , support , and inspire both the kidCEO™ and the parent/s behind them.

As you turn the page to read each chapter, you will encounter an interior decorator who helped decorate a celebrity's nursery, to a teen who is the CEO of a call center that answers the phones for Disney, and many more. These kids are nothing short of amazing and are examples for generations to come. The Keys to Success and wisdom shared in this book have proven results.

I promise you each chapter provides guidance and wisdom to help you and your kid start the journey to entrepreneurship. I wish you well in your own entrepreneurial journey and look forward to you joining the kidCEO™ club!

Yours in entrepreneurship,

Jennifer H. Gormer

"My mission in life is not merely to survive, but to thrive; and to do so with some passion, some compassion, some humor, and some style."
~ Maya Angelou

Jennifer Hobson Gormer

Jennifer Hobson Gormer

BUSINESS NAME
NextGen Fusion Call Center

kidCEO™
Alexius McCoy

ESTABLISHED
2016

MISSION
NextGen Fusion Inc virtually supplies part-time and full-time work for veterans, college students and stay at home parents

VISION
NextGen Fusion will be internationally known for businesses small and large to use to employ virtual customer service representatives.

NexGen Fusion supplies work for those who work from home and provides quality work for companies in need of customer service.

The Serial Entrepreneur kidCEO™

In August 2016, my father decided to leave. At that time I had passive income streams from my vending machine business, J's Vending, in honor of my brother's genius, and Super Sitter, my babysitting agency. Unfortunately, having a vending machine business was very time consuming and I was also moving out of state, which meant that no one would have been checking the machines and that's not okay. My babysitting business wasn't going to work either because I couldn't watch the kids from 600 miles away. So, I sold my vending machines and helped my family instead move to a new place. After all was said and done, I knew I needed to help my mom with her new bills. Emotionally, I wasn't ready to get a job again, especially one that required me to commute back and forth.

That's when I heard about virtual call centers. I worked for one and I was hooked. It was a no-brainer to work for a virtual call center because I was able to pick the schedule that I wanted, which allowed me to help with the things that my mom needed, such as groceries and running errands. I also wanted to help other people have that level of flexibility. So I created

NextGen Fusion Inc., a virtual call center. I came up with the name because I wanted to bring both young and old into the virtual customer service realm.

As a serial teen entrepreneur I believe that I am an original because creating NextGen Fusion wasn't my first business. However, it was the first successful business that I started by myself to help my family when things were at its lowest. You see my other businesses, vending machines, face painting, babysitting, and mascot work were primarily just for fun. I was also able to help my mom, if needed, with some things, to an extent. Fortunately, with NextGen Fusion I was able to do so much more. I was truly able to contribute to the household including picking us up, paying bills in full, and having money leftover just in case anything additional happened or was needed. I remember in the beginning of starting NextGen Fusion that I worked most of the day. I didn't make time for much else because my family needed the money to get us into our own home and out of my grandparent's spare room. When we moved into our brand new place, we only had our laptops and clothes so we had to get moving.

At first, I worked from 7 a.m. to 5 or 6 p.m. every day to get people into my business and make sure they received training. I also conducted training with other companies to see how they worked, what the instructors were like, and what was a good match and/or candidate. All of the companies I trained with had a different way of training so I kept that in mind during my interviewing processes. At one time I had 285 candidates and only one me! I panicked! But after a few hours of trying to figure it out and finally asking for help, I got an answer to my problem. We live in an amazing age of technology to make it easy to reach people quickly! And that's exactly what I did. I sent a brief message to the candidates asking for their contact information to receive further instructions from me.

You would be amazed how many people can't follow simple instructions and they were the ones who I eliminated from my list. I eventually got the applicant list down to 120 applicants, of which fifty complied. I can tell you now that growing my business didn't happen overnight. It took me about five months to get to where I am now because of the challenges of finding the right people to fit my company's needs. Fortunately, I am now able to get on top of things and I can make myself available twice a month to do payroll. I work approximately 15 to 25 hours a week and volunteer the other parts of the day.

I enjoy hanging out with my family during the evening and some weekends when I am not hanging out with my friends. I try to make sure I budget my time because I tend to be a workaholic. I love working hard, doing research, and getting to know more people who want to work for me. I'm also more conscience of my time because when I was younger I didn't take much time for myself between my business, school, homework, and chores. I honestly didn't think I needed time to relax, but now I have a set schedule which allows me to make time to do what I love to do, such as going swimming and playing football or basketball with my friends. I also have plenty of time to do the dishes, mop

"When you pour yourself into your business or whatever you plan to do, it's no longer about how much you make, but what you learned and how you can use what worked or didn't work in the future."

the floors, and clean my room!

The biggest challenge in being a kidCEO™ is finding something that you enjoy and making it work for you. I enjoyed all of my past businesses. I love to give back to the community in any way that I can, and by having vending machines, painting faces, and taking pictures with kids I was able to give money to charities and hospitals. All of my businesses were created to help others in one way or another, which is my true joy. NextGen Fusion allows me to help people successfully work from home while helping businesses that need great people to work for them remotely. I also enjoy leading people and helping them see that they have so much more potential than a traditional 9 to 5 job. Allowing my contractors to flourish without me standing over their shoulder and making sure they are doing what they need to do is amazing. I picked up those skills from my mother. She is a natural leader and people love being around her to build whatever she believes in. She never gives up and neither do I. I will not settle for second place. I stand tall because I know I'm a winner.

Lessons Learned

The first businesses I started on my own did not end very well. In fact, I would say that it ended badly. I wanted to start a business for and about cars, via an App. I had just finished a high school mechanics class and I noticed that I was one of two girls in class. I figured if only two of us were in that class, then there were a lot of girls who knew nothing about cars. I wanted to help those girls, or guys, get a simple understanding of their cars without getting ripped off by the "professionals". I enjoyed the process of coming up with the App but I quickly realized that I did not know everything I needed to know to fully bring the concept to life. I had the vision, but not the technical skills to get my App from my brain to the App store.

I have a lot of ideas so I make sure to write them down because I don't want to keep them locked away in my brain and never come to fruition like the car App. I eventually learned that just because I don't know how to code HTML and Java with precision it doesn't mean that I can't find someone who does. I tried to teach myself code in order to build the App but it turned out

I am really great at making balls move across a screen. I was determined to code the App myself to see what I could do. I have to admit that I'm a Do-It-Yourself kind of person. I love getting my hands dirty and getting an understanding of the projects that I want to conquer inside and out.

My mother always had my brother and I keep notebooks that we called success journals. We wrote down what went well, questions we want answered, and/or how we were doing that day. It's designed to keep all of our growth, failures, and ideas in one place. What I learned from my application building days was that sometimes you need a team to help you where you lack.

Another adventure I embarked upon was being an entertainer. What started out at my mom's old balloon twisting business then upgraded to a face painting and balloon twisting business that transformed into a mascot business! As a mascot I enjoyed entertaining kids of all ages, even the occasional adult. I had so much fun dressing up and playing around. Dancing was my favorite part, second only to the surprised looks and giggles on my host's faces! I got to go all out into a character. If I was a strapping mouse, then I played the mouse with class. If I was a cute kitty, then I skipped as often as I liked. But when I started doing it all by myself with my own costumes, instead of renting, I noticed that I didn't have enough clients on a monthly basis. Birthdays only come once a year so eventually I learned that scheduling and building a fan base or clientele are crucial in the entertainment business, especially if you love having fun every other day.

With my babysitting business, I made sure to take a babysitting class when I was 12-years-old. This was the first business that I ran all by myself. But as I got older, I noticed the parents were taking advantage of my very low prices. They often wanted me to work longer hours. With that and other inconveniences, I created contracts for them to sign because my time was more valuable. The lesson I learned from babysitting was creating a contract that detailed my work time and pay. You should always have a contract because business between you and your clients works best with a clear and concise contract.

With my vending machine business, I learned many things, but the most important things included start small, keep records, and keep a good schedule. Nothing is more embarrassing that an empty machine. When I was graciously handed the keys to the machines from my younger brother, I kept the same amount of machines so I could get a feel for it. Once I understood how to schedule and get the most out of the candy in each location, I purchased more machines and put them in new locations. It was a great feeling to expand but there were days when I had to rush to fill machines.

With my call center, I have learned that making a good work environment for myself and my contractors are important. I made sure my workspace is clean, and I send reminders to my employees with the same information. A clean desk is a happy desk! I also make sure they are paid on time, so they don't have to guess when their next check will come in. When I know what I am doing and can better assist my clients, it makes everyone happy. I do this by always being on time. "Always be early, never be late, makes a CEO smart, pretty, and great."

It's like going to school… if you are always late to class you fall behind. In the business sense, you either lose clients or employees. Both are bad … kind of like

Keys To Success

As a kidCEO™ I am the leader and my employees look up and follow my example. You need to be that leader.

1. Be A Leader. (Virtual Call Center interviews)
2. Know What You're Worth. (Vending machines)
3. Always Have A Contract. (Babysitting)
4. Make Time To Have Fun. (Mascot)

Raising A Serial Entrepreneur kidCEO™

I let Alexius, my kidCEO™ know that she can do anything she puts her mind to. Our motto is "If you can perceive it, then you can conceive it." or "If it's going to be, it's up to me."; Whichever fits the mood or occasion. Also, I let Alexius know it's okay to make mistakes, as these are life lessons that teach us what didn't work and what we need to do differently to achieve the outcome we want. I've had to work at finding balance between being the sounding board for Alexius and being her nurturing mother and shoulder to cry on. I think all loving parents can agree that we want our kids to succeed. However, as the parent we also have to protect our kids from anything we regard as dangerous, whether the child believes it's so or not; we MUST protect our precious cargo until we have to let them go. So in finding balance as the "mom-ager" I've had to make time to help Alexius put together a goal chart and one-by-one we discuss which ones have the best chance and how each will affect her time and pocketbook. We can have all the dreams in the world, but if we can't get anyone else to see the vision it remains a dream.

We also talk about the "realistics" of the vision or

dream to see if it will be able to have a fighting chance. Another thing I do is lower the hammer when I feel that she's had enough. Alexius can sometimes breathe life into something so long that it appears to be working, but in reality it's just SUCKING the life out of her. Then after we've had time to refocus I kick into mom mode with the encouragement that she can rise again, just like a Phoenix. And to my delight, she does.

I have Alexius keep a Notebook of Success. This is a journalography of things that she is working on, has worked on, and will work on, as well as what worked with certain projects and what didn't. It's a road map that keeps her focus clear. I look at it like a guide that takes her through the tough times whether I'm around or not. Alexius also uses the "Success Notebook", for school, other events in her life, and her entrepreneurial endeavors. I feel that Alexius is better equipped when she has something to reference from and then she can fix things as she goes forward. The notebook also helps her from spinning her wheels with things that need to be visited later. For the best example of what the success notebook looks like and the flow of it please visit: http://bit.ly/MySuccessNotebook.

When I do not know the answer, I find someone in my network who does. I believe as parents we know a lot about a lot of things but we don't know everything nor do we need to. Just be the resource to get the answers. I follow the wise adage, "I don't need to know everything; I just need to know where to find it, when I need it".

I encourage her to explore options that are not always traditional. "Think outside the box". Let me elaborate on what I mean for just a moment. Alexius was once told she could not perform as a particular popular character when she owned her mascoting business. The verbiage was along the lines of the exact "Name" that was branded and trademarked and could not be used in advertisements. So, she changed the name to describe what the character was. And that little change was enough to let her continue to perform and make money as she originally intended. Finding the solution or resolving the issue or just dropping the issue are all options at a parent's disposal. If we are fearless, driven, or calm as a cucumber, then our kidCEO™'s will be also.

Building up her inner and outer self and not allowing anyone to tell her that it can't be done, has allowed Alexius to understand the strength that she has to keep moving forward. I have always taught my children "cause" and "effect" which enables them to become critical thinkers. When commercials would come on I'd ask, "Alexius, what are they trying to sell us?"

After her response I'd ask, "What was a few good selling points and what wasn't effective?"

Finally I'd ask, "How would you have done it differently?"

She became armed with questions and objectives to see the outcome of certain situations before they happened. When she is told no and she's passionate behind what she wants to do, she digs in to make it happen.

Let me give you a true to life experience. Alexius wanted to put her logo on a race car to help kids with various ailments. She wanted to know who to contact to make this happen and I helped her find people who could can help. Unfortunately, she was told, "No," by a few, some didn't respond at all, and others thought that it was a wonderful idea but left it at that. All the Nos and naysayers meant nothing to her. The only one who mattered was the race car driver who finally said "YES!"

Sometimes you have to push through barriers to get the answer you want. This is why I remind her of the Bessie Coleman's of the world. The people who were told No a lot, but persevered to their "YES" are the ones written in our memoirs. To sum it up, if someone tells Alexius "NO" you can't do this or that, we simply tell them to prove it!

Lessons I've learned through trial and error while raising a kidCEO™ are as follows:

1. As parents we use words to impress upon the minds of our colleagues and peers our thoughts and feelings. Kids aren't peers or colleagues, so we need to put the information in kid-friendly terminology so that they understand the legal terms and obligations, while not suppressing the creative person inside.

2. I try very hard to make time in my schedule to be the soundboard when the creative juices

are flowing for Alexius, EVEN when it's late at night.

3. I work hard to remember my kidCEO™'s feelings from a mom's perspective and not always from a business perspective.

4. I remember how it was to be young with great ideas that most other people didn't get. As parents of these wonderful gifted youths, just be there, show up, and let them know you care.

5. Oh and this is very important. "Hey a girl's gotta sleep sometimes." But really and seriously, take care of yourself so that you can take care of your kidCEO™.

Jennifer's Notes

I found Alexius via Facebook. At first, it was hard to know whether Alexius was a kid or not because she is such a professional. She is determined, brilliant, and resilient. Having learned that the teen was a serial entrepreneur before the age of 18, Alexius had to tell her story in kidCEO™. She is definitely an inspiration for those youths who want to start more than one business.

Jennifer Hobson Gormer

BUSINESS NAME
Precious Designs | PDesignsTX

kidCEO™
Jasmine Benton

ESTABLISHED
2012

MISSION
My mission is to be the inventive mind through creative redesign of client's furnishings and exceptional customer experience.

VISION
Exceptional Redesigns of Client Treasures

BUSINESS STATEMENT
Precious Designs is an interior decorating business. I refurbish and re-design housewares such as chairs, ottomans, side tables, pillows, vases, trays, stools, and more. I also sell products on my website. I have several key services, which are:

- Re-designing and refurbishing furniture
- Decorating and Designing Events
- Designing rooms in homes
- Personal Furniture Shopping Service

PRECIOUS *pd* DESIGNS

The Interior Decorator kidCEO™

When I was 9-years-old, my grandma decided that I could go with her to her client's homes. My grandma is an interior decorator and her first degree was in interior design. My grandma refurbished old furniture and redesigned the home to feel as if IKEA designed the space. When I got to tag along, I became her assistant. She taught me design styles and techniques while redesigning her client's homes. Because of those experiences with my grandma I learned how to arrange furniture, determine the quality of furniture, find the right color scheme, properly refurbish furniture, and much more. In fact, my grandma and I eventually started designing pillows and chairs.

Naturally I started designing whenever I could and before I knew it, design took over my life. After two years of tagging along with my grandma I told my mom I wanted to have my own design store. I created a plan, I decided on a name for my store, and I made a list of furniture that I wanted to refurbish and resell. My mom then took me to different vendor stores at a small location to open my first store. We drove around for an entire day looking until we found a space at the Allen Antique Mall.

Once I found the right space, I had to purchase my merchandise. My mom took me to a city garage sale called+ Trinkets for Treasure, where I purchased most of my merchandise. I revisit every year to buy merchandise to refurbish. For the past five years it has become a family tradition between my mom, grandma, and I. I instantly started to redesign and refurbish the furniture to resell. I had so much inventory for my store that it took me two weeks to open. It was my grand opening and I was excited because I designed the look of my store, furniture tags, marketing, and set the prices for my merchandise.

My story is unique because my grandma helped me turn my hurt and anger of my parents separating when I was nine into something beautiful. She helped me cope with the pain and confusion I was feeling. Don't get me wrong, God gave me a beautiful talent. My grandma helped me to find my passion and talent, however. When I design, I know I can show others, no matter what happens in life you are worth more than what people think. Even if you feel as if you are not going to be understood, know you are precious. That's why I named my business Precious Designs, because I wanted to share that what is within is beautiful.

Time Management

When I first started out as a business owner, I did not know how to manage my time. I was a 6th grader trying to keep my grades up and keep my passion alive. It was not easy because 6th grade was not my brightest year. However, I learned that an agenda was there to help me, not to collect dust. I started to mark down the times I needed to work on my business, as well as the times I needed to step back and be a kid. Fortunately I had two different agendas to help me stay on track. One for school and the other for my business. These items were very important in my life. In my house school was the main priority, well God is first but school was next. If I was failing one class, my mom reminded me that she could and would take away my internship with Mikel Welch and put my business on hold.

For me, my biggest challenge being a kidCEO™ is keeping my faith in my business. I love my business and I love to design however, I am extremely busy. My life was and is not your typical high schooler's life, I was enrolled in AP classes for French, English I and II, Geometry and History, which require two things: studying and lots of studying. Plus, don't forget the projects. Many kids strive to get a passing grade, but I strive to be an all A Honor Roll student. I am naturally an overachiever. I am thankful I have a strong support system in my mom, who is very proud of me and puts everything she has into her kidCEO™. With such a busy schedule I lose faith and energy trying to work on a business.

The Making Of A kidCEO™

As a young child I did not always listen to the wisdom around me from people who were trying to support and lift me up. This taught me an important lesson. As I mentioned before, I had not mastered time-management. One day my mom told me to come out to the garage, which is where my design studio is. She was upset because I had projects that I started and had not finished. I had products that I needed to refurbish and resell to make a profit. In other words, I was sitting on the profit for my business, and I needed to manage my time to get it done. This is when my mom suggested that I move my business on-line instead of running my store because it would be less time consuming and I could make money while I was in school.

When I first had my booth, I was very successful. During my grand opening I almost sold out of all the merchandise I had. My first month I sold a dining room set, anottoman, chairs, storage stairwell, and pillows; all within hours of opening my store. The owner of the Antique Mall said I was making more than most of the adults who were renting space. After that my mom became my bank, lending me money to make purchases for my business. I had to pay my loans back on time and sometimes with interest. My mom taught me the process to apply for a loan with a bank and I will never forget it.

In the beginning of my business, I did not understand my content, and it caused me to lose some business. My content is my 'What?' - What my business does and the service it provides. I needed to understand my content before promoting it to others. I also had to learn how to budget. I struggled with calculating the budget and what to do with it. Last November I refurbished an antique rocking chair for a client and the results were fabulous. However, I undercharged and my profit was very low. I did not correctly add up the costs of my materials before giving the quote for the antique rocking chair. This experience taught me to have a list of prices for every service I provide.

Keys To Success

These are some simple Keys to Success for kids who are thinking of becoming a kidCEO™ like me:

1. Build yourself. Because you are the founder of the company it helps if you take classes or get a certificate that legally allows you to do what you want to do.
2. Planning. Schedule your day-to-day tasks and activities because every day you need to do something for your business. Don't do the same thing everyday.
3. Serve others. There is nothing better than

using your company, in the right way, to serve your community.

4. Listen to wisdom. Adults are around us for a reason so listen to them, because if you do not you will eventually find out they were right.

From MeeMaw to Jasmine - A Shared Vision

My support began long before there was even an idea of being a CEO or owner of a business. My support was igniting the dream and sharing the knowledge of a design dream that was not possible during my youth, growing up during an era when African-Americans had limited opportunities. Growing up in the projects, as a young girl, I knew that I could only be a teacher, nurse, and/or work as a domestic helper, like my aunt. She received a subscription to *LIFE Magazine* with wonderful pictures of wonderful fashions and beautiful interiors. As a result, my mother would attempt to recreate some of the beautiful designs in our home. Our living room became a laboratory of design projects. We refurbished, redesigned, and recovered the furniture and accessories twice a year – every spring and fall, with the season's new colors as dictated by *LIFE Magazine*.

I learned how to make drapes, and re-upholster sofas and chairs. I dreamt of becoming an interior designer and studied design in college for the first two years where I learned about fabrics and patterns. Later I switched to business studies to support myself.

Over the next 25 years, I used my home as a design laboratory, where I continued to feed my passion. Years later, my granddaughter happily tagged along with every treasure hunt for that special fabric, or that battered chair or trunk just waiting for a new purpose or fabulous look. Pillows quickly became her go-to gifts for loved ones.

It was obvious very early that Jasmine had developed my mother's love of interiors and my creativity.

One of the first clues: The excitement in her eyes on the weekends when I arrived to pick her up to go "treasure hunting." She started tagging along on these excursions through inexpensive and run down thrift stores (what my budget allowed) at the tender age of 3. Treasure hunting was my solution for going shopping with very little money and a lot of imagination! We gradually increased our search to include visits monthly to the fancy neighborhoods of extensive estate sales packed with family heirlooms waiting for a new home and purpose.

Another clue: The visions she crafted out loud in

the car of what we would do to the "treasure" that we just bought. The fact that she could articulate any redesign vision at a young age was fun and demonstrated that she could see past the obvious wear and tear to the purposeful or fancy furniture that it could become. Some were based upon her love of all princess style cartoons, but others indicated an affection for the rustic and vintage look she loves to this day.

The most significant clue was her willingness to dive into the restoration and repurposing of our treasures. Whether scraping off old paint, sanding down wooden treasures, padding an old worn ottoman, or even sewing brand new accent pillows - she joined the redesign fun eagerly, and always with her own ideas. As she grew more experienced and confident, she developed her own ideas, vision, style, and plans. Sometimes, we differed on the ideas - but that only added to the final product. We continued to tackle harder projects, and bought countless design magazines. Together we have created a design reference library that she will hopefully take with her to a university's design program.

The Hardest Lessons

For a grandparent, the hardest lesson is learning how to allow them to make choices and decisions that you know will have unfortunate results. With the benefit of experience, you want to help them avoid some of the pitfalls bad choices or decisions may cause. For example, my granddaughter called with exciting news. She had accepted a client project to refurbish an early American rocking chair that was a cherished family heirloom. The client wanted the seat repaired with new upholstery and the wood painted. She had negotiated a price that the client accepted.

As I congratulated her, I began to ask questions and my concerns grew with every response. I quickly realized that she was going to need extensive help in order to meet the promised deadline of two weeks. I decided to use the project as a teachable moment. At the end of the two weeks, we had tracked the number of overtime hours and created a master list of tools needed for future projects. The final tally: We had a beautifully completed project, a happy client, enhanced knowledge, and a small profit. My granddaughter was proud of what she accomplished. She had learned some very key lessons that would aid her with future design clients, including:

- Use a consistent method to price products and your service
- Keep a detailed list of all expenses, including labor hours
- Know the difference between revenue and profit for your product or service

My granddaughter wasn't the only one who learned from the experiences. As grandparents, we aid, support, educate, and nurture. For me, it was hard to not step in and help. I would have happily called the customer of the family heirloom, an Early American rocker, and renegotiated the pricing on her behalf. However, there was a personal reward for not stepping in. What was the reward? It allowed me to watch her grow, develop, and gain confidence based on understanding and actual experience with her own customer. I saw the growth and the understanding increase. I saw the "light bulb" moment that teachers, trainers, facilitators, and presenters all know and recognize when the audience "gets it." Seeing the light bulb moment as we debriefed the completed, awesome redesign project… THAT was an awesome experience.

In summary, what would I do differently? What lessons learned do I have? What advice can I share with others who want to see their children or grandchildren begin to take the entrepreneural road trip? Honestly, I can sum it up in just a few words:

- Encourage
- Explore
- Start Small

For my granddaughter, what started as an inexpensive way to spend time together turned into a shared passion. Starting small at the inexpensive corner thrift stores and down the back alleys on trash pickup day in the suburbs. As she displayed an interest in my lifelong passion that I shared with my mother, I chose to encourage her. I gained just as much from her youthful vision and exploring nature as she did from my experience.

We explored other avenues as money and time allowed. The dreams and the projects kept getting larger. That larger dream and experience gave her the courage to quickly seize an unexpected opportunity to introduce herself to a renowned interior designer that we happened to see in a crowded hallway of a convention center. She gleefully introduced herself and instantly connected with the designer with her love of interiors. She managed to make a connection that few people have a chance to make, and it grew into an unexpected internship opportunity unheard of by grown adults, let alone a teenager. That is the beginning of her journey and I can't wait to see the next stop.

Jennifer's Notes

Jasmine is part of the reason that kidCEO™ exists. Jasmine is my daughter and started her business, opening her own store at age 11. She helped design Steve Harvey's grandson's nursery and interned with Mikel Welch of HGTV. She has inspired many kids and I decided to create a solution for kids that want to start a business and don't know how.

Jennifer Hobson Gormer

BUSINESS NAME
Aplomo Couture

kidCEO™
Celeste Johnson

ESTABLISHED
2016

MISSION
Help One Of a Kind Women Create their One Of A Kind Dress

VISION
Aplomo short-term is a quickly growing runway presence inspired by the small nuances of life. Long-term Aplomo is in two forms: Not only on the runway, but also an on-line platform where women can go to collaborate with Aplomo Designers and create the dresses of their dreams.

BUSINESS STATEMENT
One Of A Kind Women Deserve One Of A Kind Dresses. Aplomo provides these dresses through an innovative on-line and in-person experience catered to the individual woman.

The Fashion Designer kidCEO™

One-of-a-kind women deserve one-of-a-kind dresses, but how can someone build a business from such a simplistic phrase. Honestly, it was just a childhood hobby, something to hold a young 10-year-old's attention long enough for her parents to catch their breath. That is until she was introduced to Project Runway™ and suddenly dress forms and a constant stream of sewing supplies was a must.

The moment that Aplomo shifted from hobby to business began with Aplomo's first public appearance at the Fashion X Dallas Fashion show in September of 2016. From there things took off with an entrepreneurship class at Coppell High School that allowed for a dream to gain some realistic goals, knowledge, and lifelong connections ensuring my next steps were smart ones. The class was incredibly flexible and allowed to me to continue to have a job outside of school without falling behind in my studies. By the time I had decided to join the class, just about everyone who knew me knew exactly why. I had made it a point to be very open about my business and had even been receiving requests for custom dresses now and then. You see, officially Aplomo became a business once it was showcased publicly. However, personally Aplomo became a business the minute I decided to lead a life based on my passion as a one-of-a-kind, self-taught fashion designer.

Yes, you read that right, completely self-taught from the age of 10. My grandmother and aunt showed me the basics of sewing and my great grandmother, who had been a seamstress made it a point to take the opportunity to empty her sewing closet whenever I visited; not that I was complaining any. My dad noticed the potential and would make me hand sewn dresses whenever my sister and I visited him. I believe it was for Christmas that he and my step-mom gave me a bin of fabric, patterns, a dress-form, and a sewing box. I was overjoyed at the time. However, as much love for my new found hobby that I had, there is nothing quite like having to sew an entire dress together by hand at an age when my attention span wasn't much longer than a couple minutes.

Of course, my Dad forced me to not waste fabric when cutting out pieces, seeing as he obviously wasn't planning on getting me any more. Keeping in mind the spirit of being self-taught, he also had me look up what all the little notations, markings, and words meant on the patterns. If I didn't know it off the top of my head, I had better pick up my tablet, take notes, and practice before even thinking to ask him. YouTube videos, blog posts, picture tutorials, etc. are the basis of what I know now. At the time I was annoyed of course, but that tough love has given me much more drive to find things out for myself, which in the end benefitted me incredibly.

In terms of next steps, smart meant anything but easy. Between conceptualizing and sketching designs at school, then coming home and immediately putting together the pieces, I had next to no free time. I learned the hard way that there needed to be a "work-life balance" as my mom had anxiously informed me many times. As I'm sure you can understand, it can be hard to listen to parents, it especially was and still is for me. I'm normally the kind of person who has to find things out for herself, even if it means testing out what does and doesn't work. For example, staying up working on homework, a collection, and an on-line college course essay all at the same time for a straight week just doesn't work out; Something my mom warned me about. Trust me, it's easier to listen to a just a few things they say.

It was a challenge to identify what I was able to handle within certain periods of time while also allowing for proper relaxation and sleep, especially since senior year meant sleep was already a small priority. However, my biggest challenge was and continues to be my bad time management skills. After testing out many at-home remedies to this bad habit, I have found that keeping an organizer, of some sort, handy at all times works the best. I like to keep a bullet journal, because it allows much more freedom to organize my thoughts as I please in a creative way that I enjoy. I try to keep my schedule up-to-date and documented in order to keep myself focused on the task at hand without losing sight of future upcoming tasks. This leads into what I have learned from my experience in building Aplomo.

Lessons Learned

Even though it may suck, it's incredibly important to learn from one's failures. A major lesson I learned the hard way starting Aplomo as a young kidCEO™, is to not be afraid to ask for help and to know one's limits. Contracts are serious agreements that could turn sour quickly if not handled correctly. When considering to sign a contract with an individual or organization, it is crucial to make sure that all the key components of a stable contract are there. If you don't and something doesn't go as planned or someone doesn't fulfill their side of the agreement, the contract will not be able to keep them on the hook as needed. Aplomo had signed a contract without having it looked over by an adult, which resulted in the other party taking advantage of my overall inexperience and a very large amount of money was lost. This could have been prevented if I had asked my parents or another outside adult to look over the contract before I had signed it. That was the point at which I recognized that I can't do it all by myself. It was in fact a learning process.

At the other end of the spectrum, it's essential to learn from successes as well. Aplomo has participated in three fashion shows, Fashion X Dallas 2016, Fashion X Austin 2017, and the 2017 Asian Mint Fresh Asian Fusion Fashion Show in Dallas. I was the youngest designer in both the Fashion X Dallas and Asian Fusion Shows and interviewed at all three shows as well. From these fashion shows Aplomo has gained many more connections and opportunities, which in turn has led to more shows and larger audiences. One great example of this is the fact that Aplomo is a part of this book, kidCEO™. Aplomo learned of this opportunity from a connection made at the 2017 Asian Mint Fresh Asian Fusion Fashion Show.

From these shows, I learned that no one is going to believe in your idea if you do not make it apparent that you do. Confidence is key. Don't let talking in front of others scare you. I remember how nervous I was when faced with networking for the first time. I learned from my step-mom and Dad to take it slow, write down the key points of your business, and memorize them, and when answering questions focus on those points so that your sentences and thoughts are consistent. With practice, networking will feel as natural as gossiping with friends.

Keys To Success

Here are a few key things I try to remember:

1. If you have any doubts when building your business, then talk to someone or research how others did what you are looking to do. It's always best to have all the information before making any decision no matter how small.

2. Have a reason for everything you do. Whether it's an event or a photo shoot, think ahead: How will it advance your business both short-term and long-term? Is this something you are getting paid for or something you just want to try out? In

what way will it benefit your business?

3. Don't be afraid to ask for help. Right now you can't do everything by yourself and that's okay. If anything, take advantage of your resources, including your parent's resources, whoever it may be because when you get older figuring it out will all be on you.

4. Last but not least, don't be afraid to change your mind. If you find that you don't want to run your business anymore, then ask for help and mentors who can support you in achieving your dreams. In the end it's your life. It would suck to be stuck in a business that you no longer have any passion for and honestly, that defeats the purpose of you becoming the entrepreneur that you are!

So that's my story. Things to remember: know your limits, ask for help, be confident, research is your friend. Think ahead, and don't tie yourself down to something you don't absolutely love. In my case, it's Aplomo, an incredibly customizable on-line and in-person dress designing experience tailored to the one-of-a-kind woman and it's my lifelong dream-turned-reality that I hope you can learn and take away from.

Raising A Fashion Designer kidCEO™

Since I am her mom first before anything else, my priority is to help her learn what work-life-balance works best to meet both her personal and professional goals. She must learn how to see the decisions that have a positive long-term benefit versus the impulsive decisions that may or may not fulfill a short-term want or need. When she was younger, my support was focused on exposing her to different perspectives and hands-on approaches to sewing, knitting, etc. and submerging her in it during her summers with family. This was followed by a week-long 40-hour workshop at FIT in New York the year of her 15th birthday. I was also focused on helping her to see that making mistakes is okay and that is how a person learns; which further developed both her and her product.

Celeste's fashion ideas and designs have been a career interest since she was very young, so when I told her that a co-worker of mine mentioned seeing if he could get her into a show, she was very excited. When that co-worker didn't come through, I was proud to watch that fire turn into applying and getting invited to show her first collection at Fashion X Dallas! Now at 17-years-old, my support for her has evolved into sharing my 15+ years of professional contract and agreement-related experience in the guidance that I provide her. It allows me to empower her to make the decisions she feels is best for her business. This includes but is not limited to using my professional contacts to help her research how to protect the Aplomo brand, my availability to review and provide feedback regarding professional correspondence, self-presentation, product presentation, tracking of business-related expenses, and other valuable resources that many businesses do not have. At the end of the day, my part is to help empower my daughter to make professional choices that are healthy for both her and her business so that she can gain her own related experience to help build a strong and confident foundation for her future decision-making skills.

It is important as a parent of a kidCEO™ to find an effective and evolving balance of knowing when to guide versus lead and protect. While they are younger, I believe that a kid should be provided the window of opportunity to see for themselves how much of an interest they do or don't have in something, while the parent protects and then nurtures that. Allow the interest to grow organically, then as they get older, guide and provide advice but empower them with decision-making. Always be willing to be fully transparent for why certain scenarios require adult intervention, but still keep them fully informed so they can continue to learn by seeing how the business is being handled. Balancing between guidance and taking a step back is the biggest challenge, but I truly believe that is the only way our kidCEO™ can grow into an effective and independent adult CEO.

Jennifer's Notes

Celeste was chosen for kidCEO™ because she is the next fashion icon. Another kidCEO™'s mom met Celeste and told me about this amazing kid designer who was featured in Austin Fashion Week, and would be a fantastic addition to kidCEO™. After a 15 minute phone call and watching a feature of her work, I knew that Celeste needed to show other girls who aspire to join the ranks of fashion designers in the national fashion world that they too can follow their dreams.

BUSINESS NAME
Professional Model and Actor

kidCEO™
Helena de Moraes

ESTABLISHED
2004

MISSION
My mission is to help brands, large and small, make their vision become more visible in the marketplace so to make a bigger impact.

VISION
My vision is to help inspire other kids to follow their dreams in this industry while making a positive impact in the world.

The Professional Model And Actress kidCEO™

It's not how you do it, it's how you live it. It's not what you see, it's how you look at it. It's not how your life is, it's how you live it. – Anonymous

It's pretty cool to see yourself on a huge billboard on Fifth Avenue in New York City and in national advertising campaigns! I am a fashion and commercial model and this is exactly what has happened to me. As a fashion and commercial model, I take pictures to advertise clothing, makeup, or accessories that show on TV and internet advertisements, print material like catalogs, or virtually on websites. As a model, I am an extension of a brand, I basically represent a company. I am the business. If I cannot be trusted, then companies in the future will not give me jobs. Lots of people think modeling is about funny and over dramatic poses but it's nothing like that. You have to be serious but at the same time have fun. You need to be comfortable in front of the camera and in front of people. Usually poses are pretty subtle and you need to have the right expressions for the photo shoot or runway.

I started modeling in 2004 when I was six months old after my parents submitted my pictures to an agency. I spent a lot of time on set and enjoyed it, but of course, as a baby and toddler, I didn't really know it was business. When I was about 5, I took a break because I no longer enjoyed modeling. I wasn't having fun anymore and it wasn't as exciting as it had been. But at the age of eleven, I really wanted to get back to modeling because I thought it would be fun to try again. Two things reignited my passion. My best friend was modeling for the same agency as I did before and was participating in a fashion show called Fire & Ice. In Fire & Ice we had to train beforehand. We learned how to walk the runway and what order we would be going in and we were told what clothes we would be modeling in. The person who was teaching us how to do these things was the leader of kidCEO™, Mrs. Jennifer Gormer. I knew I wanted to do more because I enjoyed it so much.

I also wanted to challenge myself in confidence and interpersonal skills. Modeling challenges you to put yourself in front of people and teaches you poise. When I was younger, I had a pretty low self-esteem. I cried over some of the smallest things, like not getting to watch TV later at night, not getting a certain toy, or getting scared. Long story short, I was a wimp. Modeling and acting helped me build up my confidence and character as a person. To restart my modeling career, my mom helped me submit my photos to an agency. We used professional photos that were a good example of a head shot and a full body shot. We mailed the photos requesting agency representation. The waiting was pretty agonizing but one day I received a call for a meeting for an audition where I read a script and acted for them. They invited me to come back!

To prepare for modeling, I did a lot of theater work. At my old elementary school, there was a club where we learned how to do plays. We would learn how to memorize our script, project our voice, and how to move correctly. I also went to certain camps but one that I really enjoyed was the one Chris Ann Say was teaching. Chris is a producer which means she calls us in to audition for commercials. She is the nicest and most upbeat person you will ever know. It's almost like nothing can bring her down. She is an amazing teacher and is great with kids. She taught us how to walk the runway, poses you do in a shoot, act for commercials, dance, and so much more! At home I would research a bit more about how modeling works or what types of modeling there were.

To model, you need to be in shape. The way I get in shape is I do lots of sports and exercising. At school I do athletics which is like a more hardcore PE or I'll do a workout camp. We do weight room, running a couple miles, sprints and other things. I do as much volleyball as I can and this year it payed off and I made the volleyball team. I also do pole vaulting which requires a lot of upper body strength. When I eat I try to get all the colors of the rainbow. At school when I buy lunch, I try to get healthy things or when I bring lunch I have different fruits and vegetables and maybe a sandwich. But of course I'll have a little bit of dark chocolate.

To prepare for modeling, on the way I usually will give myself a pep talk or do a power pose for a minute. There is no reason to be nervous or scared because everyone there is going to be helping you do this job. They will tell you you're doing a great job or if you're stuck on what pose to do next they might tell you to do this or that next.

My story is unique because I decided to become

more visible and be in front of people. I needed to take a leap of faith to be more successful to grow and follow my dream. I've always wanted to be an actress, but becoming a model seemed like the first step. The more I modeled the more I wanted to do it and that's when it became my dream. I have learned to be more flexible because shoots and auditions can be last minute. For example, I can be going about my daily life and then I get a call from my booking agent telling me I have an audition, call back, or job tomorrow. I try to always be aware and ask the booking agents to schedule me outside of school time so that I don't miss too much school.

Lessons Learned

My biggest challenge is not knowing when the next audition or job is going to be. The waiting can be very frustrating. With the money not being consistent you have to learn to be okay with ambiguity. You may get a job every few days, or an audition every few months. What I learned from my failures is that not every job is your job. When you go for an audition, you need to keep in mind that you are not the only person going for the job. More than likely, there will be over 100 other people auditioning for the same print ad, commercial, or runway opportunity. I once had an audition for a SAG (Screen Actors Guild) commercial for Ford. I even got the call back, but I didn't get the job. I had to get over the disappointment, especially since a really good friend got the job instead. I stayed positive.

Keys To Success

If you are a kid who wants to become a professional model, my advice is for you is:

1. Don't give up on your career. Just keep trying because there will always be other jobs.
2. Just be yourself. Your business is your personality so it's very important to be yourself. Show the directors you can follow directions and at the same time put a little of your own personality into the audition.
3. It's important to be confident, but not to have a big ego. The difference between the two is:

being confident is being sure of yourself and having an ego is thinking you are better than everyone else. If you lead with your ego, then you will be disappointed. You can't depend on outside validation. You have to draw from a source within, which is your confidence.

I learned from my successes that I cannot rest on my laurels. What this means is that you are so satisfied with what you have already done, you make no further effort to do more. If I rely on my successes alone without continuing to hone my craft, then I won't continue getting jobs. Through my successes I have had to learn how to act and conduct myself professionally and interact in a mature way. Examples of being professional include, being polite, having a good character, and respecting others.

Raising A Model And Actress kidCEO™

I can remember it like it was yesterday. It was the day Helena was born. We were filled with joy, amazement and awe of our little girl, especially the full head of hair she had! This child had so much hair that by the time she was two months old, she looked like she had a bob hair cut! It was so unreal that when I put her in her Baby Bjorn, facing the front, people seriously thought I was carrying a doll!

At that point, I was a professional dancer, actor, and university professor, so it was only natural for me to consider bringing her into the industry, especially with her adorable demeanor and looks. She had, and still has, the ability to pass for different ethnicities, which I believed would be beneficial. That belief has paid off. At six months, after submitting photos to one of the top modeling agencies in the southwest region of the US, we were called in for her to be seen, and ultimately, invited to be represented by them.

Immediately she started working, modeling for such companies as JCPenney and Hewlett-Packard, appearing both on-line and in print. In order to support her in this journey I made sure that my schedule could be flexible by making the decision to work for myself by creating my own business. This industry often calls for you to be able to go in the very next day to either audition or shoot, so it's imperative to have either a parent or someone such as a nanny to be flexible and available. I will discuss this more in a bit. When she was about four or five she lost interest, so we took a break. I always said that we would quit if one of two things happened: one, she got bored, or two, the other kids got catty or mean. Fortunately, number two never happened.

Once she hit age 11, she started getting the itch to get back into the industry. Her best friend was at the same agency and had continued acting and modeling since they were both babies. We resubmitted Helena and her sister's photos to the agency, and, to our joy, they both got in! As parents of two models, we want them to follow and achieve any dreams they aspire to. It hasn't always been easy as we've had to sacrifice our time to place this journey as a priority. There have been times when I could have been with clients, but chose to take the kids to auditions and filming instead. But this is exactly why I set my business up the way it is setup. I have to try and make up for that lost work time in other ways. Another way of seeing it is that I could be making money with a client, or investing my time helping her earn money that is going to college funding anyway. Either way, it's good. Our family is my priority and because we've kept our priorities in check things have worked out pretty well. As long as you work as a team, have open communication, and are flexible with schedules, it is totally possible and plausible.

Another aspect we are aware of for her business is helping her expand her skills through acting classes and helping her to promote herself in various settings. Doing so has helped her with her confidence and professionalism, which will support her throughout her entire future, whatever direction she follows. The confidence, humility, and communication skills that she has had to develop through interacting with all different types of people in different situations, is truly a gift that I would never want to trade. And the potential of her ever having to quit because other kids, or industry professionals getting catty? I've actually been blown away by the respect and inclusiveness that everyone shares and shows each other since we've been a part of this. Of course, as parents we are always present so that we can monitor things, but we've been so impressed with all aspects of it thus far.

I would say one of the hardest lessons for me is to let Helena run this as her own business, letting her make her own decisions and mistakes. There has to be a fine balance between nudging her in the right direction and throwing her forward! I could easily be one of those crazy stage moms like on those pageant shows (especially since I have been in the business), where I do everything for her and push her to do things that she wouldn't want to do, but that wouldn't serve her in any way. I do coach her sometimes before auditions, but I have pretty much passed everything on to her, in terms of running her business. She is in charge of preparing her head shots and resumes before auditions, researching classes to take, and she takes part in doing her taxes. She pays for all of it, including her own income taxes. Doing so gives her valuable lessons that she will take with her for the rest of her life.

Another main challenge has been helping her navigate the ups and downs of entrepreneurialism in this industry. Modeling and acting can be amazing with all the glamour and experiences, but can also be super difficult and disappointing when she doesn't get the job she wants. I will say though, that all the disappointments have been worth it as she has learned valuable lessons that, again, have helped her develop the character and determination to keep moving towards her dreams no matter what. So far, she has worked for national ad campaigns like American Girl Doll, Frito-Lay, and others. For her, the sky is the limit. From our perspective, we will work hard to keep her in this mindset because her future successes hinges on what she does now!

Jennifer's Notes

Helena is one of the most beautiful, humble and hard working professionals I have ever met. For years she has honed her craft, practiced, and is now representing million dollar brands on billboards in New York. Helena is a professional model and actress, and while many people do not understand that her craft and her career is a business, Helena certainly understands. Helena was chosen for kidCEO™ to be a voice for the kid with hopes and aspirations for a life in front of the camera.

Jennifer Hobson Gormer

BUSINESS NAME
The Coolery

kidCEO™
Ashlyn Richardson

ESTABLISHED
2017

MISSION
To be fun, spunky, imaginative, and a creative ice cream dessert company that brings people together by offering high quality ice cream desserts and cool treats. Providing a variety of delicious cold dessert options, we bring joy to every customer, while creating a space to share joy with our community by giving back.

VISION
The Coolery's vision is to become a place to create joy for the employees, customers and community through a creative dessert experience.

The Start-Up kidCEO™

I started conceptualizing my business idea for The Coolery in the winter of 2016. I love to research unique foods and arts and crafts on YouTube. I started to notice a lot of unique ice cream treats that were foreign to me so I had a thought. If they are foreign to me, they are probably new to other people. I am always looking for new, fun experiences with food. Then I thought of how cool it would be to bring a variety of ice cream treats in one place to create an ice cream experience. Almost like an ice cream bakery, a place that you could go and pick out whatever type of ice cream dessert you want.

I shared my concept with my mom and told her all of the different types of ice cream options that I wanted to include. We also discussed the name of the business, and The Coolery was born. We chose The Coolery because just like a bakery, full of delicious baked treats, The Coolery will be full of cool ice cream treats. I believe this idea was birthed from my passion of sweets and art and out of my desire to make creative ice cream treats and to share them with all ice cream lovers.

The Coolery is a startup business and is currently

working towards opening a storefront location by the Spring of 2018 in Cedar Hill, TX. Even though my business is in the startup phase, there is still a lot of work that keeps me busy. I have participated in several business fairs to present my business idea and give samples of my product. I am currently booking parties and selling The Coolery apparel to raise money for the business. We also launched a crowdfunding campaign to continue raising money to open a storefront. Until the store front location opens I will continue to have pop-up shops bringing awareness to my business and selling products.

The Coolery will initially offer supersized shakes, called Freakshakes, ice cream sandwiches the size of burgers, called Ice Cream Burgers, servings of ice cream with lots of toppings, Fried Ice Cream, Ice Cream Tacos, and dragon's breath (a dessert that uses liquid nitrogen), and other frozen treats.

My story is unique for many reasons. My family always tells me the story about when I was around three years old I would climb in their laps and smell their breath. I would then ask them "what did you eat? "They would tell me something totally opposite of what they ate. I would say to them "that's not what you ate! "It didn't matter what they told me they ate I would tell them exactly what they ate and they would be so surprised. They thought it was amazing that I guessed the right food most of the time. I thought this story was hilarious when they told me about it. I don't remember doing this but I think it's kind of cool and weird at the same time. To think that, as a little girl I paid attention to food.

When I told my mom about my idea for The Coolery she thought it was the perfect business for me. This is because it allows me to enjoy so many things I love, like food, art, and creativity. I have tried other businesses concepts. My sister Jordyn and I had a tutu business called Rich Girlz Accessories, then I sold Woodtographs which are photographs in wood and also handmade laptop cases. I have always wanted to own my own business. I was 5 years old when my parents first encouraged me to express my creativity and to share my creations with others.

When I was 7 years old, I started having health issues and I missed a lot of school and spent a lot of time in the hospital until around 11 years old. Those three to four years taught me to focus on the positive. I learned ways to share joy with others. Actually, for two years on my birthday I hosted Giving Back parties. Big Love Cancer Care and Sharing Jed are nonprofits that works with the Arkansas Children's Hospital to support children and families and provide necessities and fun things like toys and coloring books. I worked with my school and other local schools and churches to encourage kids to give back to other kids. I was able to raise over $1,500 in two years and gave over 500 toys to the children because of all of the support that was given. This is when I figured out I really love to share with others. My business concept for The Coolery is not just about food, art, and creativity it's about bringing joy to others and helping them to create memories.

My Inspiration And My Goals

I look up to my grandparents James and Marjorie Hines, and Clint and Barbara Richardson who are currently or have been small business owners. I also look up to my parents Clinton and Jennifer Richardson who are entrepreneurs. Actually my family is full of small business owners on both sides and this helps to inspire me. I also admire Daymon John, from Shark Tank, because he is a successful business owner who is now investing in others to start their businesses. As a kidCEO™ I would love to be in a place someday that I can invest in other kidCEO™'s to ensure they can be successful in bringing their business to life. It is hard to be a kidCEO™ and kids need all the support they can get to be a success in an adult business world.

There is a lot of competition for most businesses but I believe Menchies is my biggest competition because they make their own frozen yogurt. This allows them to offer different flavors and change their flavors as often as they would like to. They also have many topping options to choose from. Menchies offers a great product but I don't think any of my competitors can compare to the experience that customers will have at The Coolery. I am looking forward to sharing The Coolery experience with ice cream lovers everywhere.

By the time I become an adult I would like to have franchise opportunities for The Coolery. I would love to see The Coolery locations pop up all around the United States. This will give me a lot of places to visit. The way I see it, if I grow the business I will make more money and be able to give more back to my community. My expansion plan is to expand the business so I can expand the joy.

Lessons Learned

I manage my time by planning a clear schedule of the day. Being a teenager, there are a lot of fun things to do, but I have to make sure that God is a priority, then business, family time, and friends. There are times I must solely focus on business and cannot get distracted. Being a kidCEO™ I also have to find a balance between school work and my business. They both take a lot of my time so it is challenging. Sometimes when my day gets started I don't have a lot of free time.

I learned that when you own a business you cannot do all the fun things that you want to do. You have be committed to the business, and giving up is not an option. That simply means that you never quit and must remember that building a business takes time. I haven't had any huge failures yet. I would just say that my biggest challenge has been feeling like I would never actually get the business started. This has made me frustrated because it seemed like the days, weeks, and months were passing by and I wasn't getting closer to my goal of opening.

What I learned during this time was that I have to focus on the positive, which was that things were getting done and remember that it takes a lot of time and effort to start a business. I am also very appreciative to those who have been helpful during this process. You have to remember to thank everyone who helps because you didn't get there by yourself. Don't ever forget where you started and how far you have come. It is easy to get frustrated when things move slowly. That's why it's so important to focus on all of the positive progress that you have made.

I tried to work through what I thought were slow periods by trying to focus on things that I could do. So I focused on flavor combinations for the Freakshakes. My sister Jordyn is the original Chief Mix Master and she helps me come up with flavor combinations for the products. We discuss which flavors should be the standard flavor combinations to offer the customers. Jordyn typically gives me a suggestion and I give her my opinion then decide if it should move forward to the next stage. If it does make the cut, then I decide how the shake or ice cream burgers will be garnished before the suggested products make it on our final list. This is the fun part, I love garnishing the desserts and coming up with names. We like to laugh a lot at all of the crazy things we come up with before finalizing the names of shakes and ice cream burgers. Ultimately, I want the name to be memorable and something that makes people smile. One of the shakes is called "Crazy for Cocoa". This shake was inspired by my aunt whose nickname is Coco and absolutely loves chocolate. Going through this process was one way I felt that I was making progress and it helped me to feel that I was one step closer to my goal.

Staying positive I started talking to everyone I knew about my business. I asked for advice on what was the best location and type of location such as a store front or a food truck. I asked about what type of ice cream places they liked. I asked what type of flavors they would like for The Coolery to have. I asked if they thought my concept was unique. I also asked them about any potential issues that they thought I may have in getting started. I not only talked to friends and family I talked to strangers, business owners, and anyone who would listen. I thought it was important to get different opinions and take them all into consideration. What I found was that when you ask people for their opinion they will give it to you. Sometimes I had really good conversations that sparked new ideas for me or gave me a different perspective. I took this feedback from everyone and started to focus on creating my business plan. This feedback helped me understand the things that would be important to my customers.

Approximately eight months later, my dream began to become a reality. I presented my businesses concept to Grow Desoto Entrepreneur Pitch Day for a business incubator that they were starting in Desoto, Texas. There was an application process involved and business were selected to pitch during this event. Out of all of the businesses that applied to pitch, my business was one of 25 selected. Out of the 25 there were only two business run by children selected. This application process was a new experience for me because I had to clearly communicated in the application who I was, what my business was and the commitment that I was willing to make to work and grow my business.

Thankfully, I was accepted and started planning all that was needed for that day. There was two big things to figure out. One was how my booth would look and if I would offer samples, and the other one was what I would say in the 3-minute pitch that was required. I started working with my mom to quickly plan because we were only notified less than 10 days prior to the event that I was selected. When we received the email I was so excited and thankful for the opportunity. My mom helped me focus on the most important things that I needed. She reminded me to read all of the information that was given to me about the event and to make a list of questions for us to ask.

Preparing for this event I realized there were some things that I needed to get done very quickly. My mom, Jennifer, took over planning for the booth to ensure I had everything I needed. She planned the booth around displaying Freakshakes, ice cream burgers, and toppings. She started gathering ingredients, supplies such as glasses for the Freakshakes and display items for the table. One thing that I didn't have at the time was branding materials. I consulted with Captivating Creations and Designer Brien Graham. He created my logo and other branding materials like t-shirts. Another thing I needed was people. There was no way that I could talk to hundreds of people at one time so I started asking friends and family to come help with my booth. My sister, Jordyn Richardson is one of my biggest supporters and she always helps with everything until she passes out from being so sleepy. She made sure someone was at the booth at all times to talk to people who visited the booth. There were so many people, friends, family, and even my mom's co-workers who helped me prepare for this event and I made sure to thank all of them.

Keys To Success

Remember that nothing is impossible because that Word itself has "I'm possible" in it. This is the way I choose to view life. I try to always stay positive and look for opportunities to laugh and make others laugh. I try to find things that inspire me and this keeps me motivated. I have received good advice from so many people. One great piece of advice that I received while doing a business fair at Trinity Church is to always keep my big smile.

I am also told that education is the key to my success. Another key to success is to research opportunities to pitch your business to potential customers and investors.

I go to business fairs to learn about other businesses and watch them pitch their products even if I am not participating. I think it is important to know as much as you can about your competition and also how other businesses present themselves to others. This helps me improve my presentation and communication skills and opens me up to other opportunities.

Praying is another key to my success. I feel that praying helps me get closer to God which allows me to know that my future will be good and not worry so much about it. This helps me to focus on the things I need to do today to be successful instead of worrying about tomorrow. For kids who want to be a successful kidCEO ™ like me you can follow these steps below:

1. Believe in yourself and never give up. I am sure you have heard the saying, "Try, try, and try again." There will be some failures along the way but just believe that you can and you will, if you never stop.

2. Focus on time management and make time to be with your family

3. Don't forget to have fun and be a kid.

I want to thank God for the success that I have had so far and the success I will have. I also want to thank my family which includes my parents; grandparents; great-grandmother Ruthie Richardson; Jordyn; all of my aunts, Brandy, Tenelle, Adrian, Denise, and Tasha; all of my uncles, Mark, Rodney, Tremain, Brien; and my godparents, Daron and Angela; and my god-grandparents, grandpa and grandma Nichols (Pickles) for all of their support. There is no way I would have been able to be as successful as I have been so far without their help. There have been many late night calls, preparing for events, proofreading materials, money invested, listening to my ideas, practicing my business pitch, and so many other things that have been done to help support me and my business and I am so thankful.

Raising A Start-Up kidCEO™

As parents, we support our daughter by believing in her dreams and investing time, money, and other resources into helping her pursue them. Our biggest and most valuable investment in her is giving her a strong foundation in God that she can grow from. As parents, we support Ashlyn by giving her unconditional love. We also support her as a kidCEO™ by helping her focus. Ashlyn is a very creative child that has many talents and abilities and many passions. We feel that it is important to help her center herself around what she should be focusing on accomplishing in the moment. This will ensure she meets the goals that she has set and ultimately achieve her dreams. We are also very hands on in our support which means we sacrifice our sleep, time and other things to ensure the business continues to move in the right direction.

We have experienced the challenges of parenting a kidCEO™ and also parenting a child with an illness. Parenting a child that was dealing with an illness has helped me to understand how to parent when life demands that you keep going. Helping Ashlyn balance school and other activities that she wanted to be apart of was a challenge for all of us but it taught us how to juggle even more than we ever thought we could manage. This took some compromise on our part as parents. As a mom I had to really focus on what was most important. For instance prior to Ashlyn getting sick I had very firm rules about her and her sister maintaining their chores. When Ashlyn got sick there were times that she would go to school and do other activities and not have enough energy to do anything else.

As a parent it was hard for me to find a balance in teaching her discipline and also allowing her to be a child. After some time I realized that it was more important for her to be a kid and not let this illness stop her from living her life. The chores will always be there and this was a opportunity for me to step in to support her. An opportunity to allow her to experience a full childhood without the stress of being perfect in everything.

Dealing with the illness and the effects of it was something she couldn't control. I had to learn how to make sure that the expectations I set for her didn't feel like a punishment. Taking pressure off her actually took pressure off of me. Being okay with her room not being perfect at all times helped us to prioritize what's important and live more in the moment. When you face uncertainty in life and in this case uncertainty about your child's health it teaches you to enjoy every moment and live to find joy and purpose. This mental shift was challenging but was healthy for me and for Ashlyn. It did require me to do more chores than I thought I should be doing. We all stepped in from Daddy, Mommy to big sister Jordyn we all carried more weight during this time versus adding more pressure onto Ashlyn. Personally, this period of time taught me how to relax a little which helped me enjoy life and enjoy being a parent.

During this time I learned a lot about parenting and also about endurance and strength from Ashlyn. There would be times that we were at the hospital most of the night and Ashlyn still wanted to go to school the next day. As her mom I wanted her to stay home and rest to make sure she didn't over do it, but Ashlyn insisted that she push herself to go to school. I never had to pick Ashlyn up from school because she pushed too hard. Ashlyn taught me that no matter what, she wasn't going to let anything stop her from whatever she desired in life. She also taught me to trust her to know her limits and ability to get things done.

Thankfully Ashlyn's health has greatly improved. She still deals with the illness but is able to function more normally. In spite of all of the challenges that create even more complexities, we still believe that her dreams will be successful. We will continue to work hard to support her and trust God to work out the other details. We believe in her and her ability to accomplish anything with God. Ashlyn is a tenaciously strong child that has so much God-given potential and creative ability and we are so blessed to be her parents.

Parenting any child is hard and one hard challenge as a parent of a kidCEO™ is to make sure you don't treat your child as an adult. This really boils down to monitoring balance and pressure. Owning and running a business requires a lot of responsibility and sometimes it can be overwhelming, even for adults. I think it is so important to understand that your child may be a business owner or entrepreneur but they are still a child. As a child they still need to be given space to be childish, make mistakes, be creative, get rest, and not carry the weight of the world on their shoulders because there will be plenty of time for that later on in life.

Remembering these things helps put into perspective that there is still a huge level of responsibility the parent of a kidCEO™ has to hold, to help them become successful while giving them the proper nurturing a child needs to live, thrive, and reach their full potential. It is important not to forget that being a kidCEO™ is one facet of who they are and all of the other wonderful unique aspects of them should be honored, valued, and celebrated just as much as the kidCEO™ they are becoming.

I would encourage all parents and especially parents with children with illness or disabilities to support your child's dreams. Someway and Somehow you will find the strength, resources and support you need for your child. In my opinion supporting Ashlyn's dreams is one way that I show my her unconditional love. Yes, this costs me and is a sacrifice a lot of the time but I am honored to give this gift of lovo to my child. I believe that the investments that I am making now will not only help her become successful, it will help her inspire other kidCEO™'s to reach their goals and help her leave a legacy in the world.

I would tell parents that even if you don't have experience being a business owner the support you can give to your child is really one of their keys to success. Children need their parent's support but also their love and encouragement. If you don't know how to support your child's business idea there are practical things that can be done that will increase your child's success.

1. Help your kidCEO ™ set reasonable goals in hopes that they will always over-achieve.

2. Stay positive and encourage your child.

3. Don't let your child give up on their dreams, even if they have to take baby steps celebrate all of them.

4. Allow your child to just be silly and play.

5. Seek new opportunities for you and your child to learn and get connected to resources.

6. Love them unconditionally.

All parents can offer these gifts to their children. These gifts don't require any business knowledge or that you are your child's business partner. The only thing that is required is for you to be a parent. Supporting a kidCEO™ is challenging but I believe that where there is vision there will be provision. Everything we need we already have or have access to. I believe this concept applies to parenting. As a parent we have a certain vision and desire for our children and we stay focused on that. The right resources, people, favor, and opportunities will be drawn to us to help us provide proper support for our kidCEO™.

Jennifer's Notes

Ashlyn was chosen for kidCEO™ because of her tenacity to serve others. Ashlyn took a difficult time in her life and used it to create joy in others. Ashlyn took her joy of desserts and created an experience where kids and families can come and create their own edible master pieces. Ashlyn was found at an entrepreneur event and was one of three kid entrepreneurs selling her products. Ashlyn was an easy choice for kidCEO™.

ABOUT THE AUTHORS

ALEXIUS MCCOY

Alexius McCoy, a serial entrepreneur and the owner of NextGen Fusion, an incorporated call center. NextGen has contracts with companies such as Disney, and employs employees from across the country. Alexius' goal is to bring generations together by having a virtual workplace that anyone with a computer and internet can work. Alexius has been featured in Colorado Girls Elevated and received the Young Woman of Distinction Award in 2016.

ASHLYN RICHARDSON

Ashlyn is the 13 year old owner of The Coolery, which is based in Dallas, Texas. "The Coolery" offers a variety of ice cream dessert treats creating a one-of-a-kind COOL dessert experience. Customers can choose one of the over the top flavor mixes or create their own custom masterpieces. The Coolery offers many dessert options such as "Freakshakes and Ice Cream Burgers, Ice Cream Tacos" and many other cool treats. Customers are able to select from over 16 custom flavor options and top them with over 20 toppings. The Coolery offers party packages for birthdays, corporate events and more.

CELESTE JOHNSON

Celeste is the owner of Aplomo, a couture fashion line for women's clothing. Aplomo has been featured in national fashion shows including Austin Fashion Week and numerous fashion shows in the N. Dallas region and has been interviewed and featured in many magazines and blogs such as Dallas weekly and EyeSee Beauty Magazine. Aplomo is built upon the concept that one of a kind women deserve one of a kind dresses. By creating an incredibly custom dress designing experience, both on-line and in-person, Aplomo makes these unique dream dresses a reality.

HELENA DE MORAES

At the age of 6 months Helena started her career as a professional model and actress when she signed with a prestigious agency based in Dallas, Texas. She has worked for such national and international brands in their ad campaigns such as American Girl Doll, JCPenny's, Frito Lay, and Hewlett Packard, just to name a few. She has been found on-line, in catalogs and billboards in New York City, representing million dollar brands.

JASMINE BENTON

Jasmine is the owner of Precious Designs, and Interior Decorating Boutique. Jasmine has owned her own storefront and had the pleasure of interning with HGTV's Mikel Welch, celebrity Interior Designer for Steve Harvey and the Obama's; and she assisted Mikel Welch and her work was shown on an episode of the Steve Harvey Show. Sshe has been featured in newspapers in Texas and interviewed for a national Teen Entrepreneur Academy. Jasmine is a credentialed Interior Decorator, an AP student and is currently attending Richland Collegiate High School with a 3.9 GPA.

ABOUT JENNIFER HOBSON GORMER

Jennifer Hobson Gormer is the Multi Best-Selling Author of *Shift On, Soul Talk* and *Surviving Abuse God's Way*. Jennifer is a national speaker who has keynoted and presented her research at national and international conferences, symposiums and summits.

Jennifer is the CEO of Idea 2 Profit™, a Learning and Business Development Firm that specializes in providing training, support and platforms to transform business ideas into profitable businesses. She has more than 18 years of Training and Development experience with Billion Dollar Brands and Artists. As a professor and best- selling author, Gormer has mastered the art of teaching others how to share their story.

As a Small Business Mentor and trainer, Jennier helps her clients to conceptualize their genius into products they can sellfor profit, through the Pathway to Profit™. To learn more visit http://www.ideatoprofit.com or call us at 972-275-9547.

Jennifer Hobson Gormer

CPSIA information can be obtained
at www.ICGtesting.com
Printed in the USA
BVHW011836040820
585480BV00004B/327

9 780998 880235